Hazing:

Through a Victim's Eyes

Adam Sand

For my wife Cathy, Papa, Gramma and
all my friends who supported me in
writing this book.

For all the victim's of hazing or bullying,
never give up.

With special thanks to Cass.

"We the victims must stand up and fight."

Chapter 1: Transition Stage

As many of us know, becoming an adult on our own is no simple transition. In a stage from kindergarten to junior high school, we have our parents making just about every decision that needs to be made. In this stage as kids, the decisions we make on our own involve: who our friends are, and our passion in what career field we want to have. Thinking about a career field, we change our minds constantly and we still get excited thinking about what could become of the future. We have no concept of money and what makes the world operate, we just ask our parents for money.

Now come the high school years, and its here that we as growing individuals make more decisions on our own. In this stage we still rely on parents but not as much. All of us are teenagers growing into young adult bodies. We hold down jobs, drive cars, have teenage drama and still do the activities we love, like for example sports. The four years spent in high school go by way to fast. The SAT's and ACT's are tests we take that colleges require us to have to get into. All the Homecomings and Proms along the way only add to the everlasting memories in high school. Graduation comes; you say your goodbyes, get your diploma and start planning your last summer before you start your college years.

With summer coming to an end, you find yourself at your own graduation. Its here that friends and family come to enjoy some last memories, embarrassing ones of high school and maybe moments from long before that. Party time is over and your college days are just right around the corner. With that being said, your summer is over; the car is packed and ready for you to begin your college years. The drive to the college of your choosing begins with comments like, "Are you sure you have everything ready?" or "You are sure that everything is packed because you don't want to forget anything?"

After this happens and many totally roll their eyes, you begin to hear lectures from your parents. We know ourselves, that just one final goodbye, and you're on your own starting what you hope is the career of your dreams.

In college, we are faced sometimes with situations that are so damaging to a person, one can't explain. For some, college goes great and for others it's totally different for various reasons. Take this advice about college from someone who has experienced something I hope people don't have to. Unfortunately my experience that happened to me still affects me till this day. I, Adam Sand, author of this book, am a victim of hazing. Hazing has some various definitions to it but my definition is simple: a downright, brutal act, intending to damage a person both physically and mentally. Before I tell you of being a victim, I'll explain about my transition stages.

My transition stages never were easy for me. I started my pre- school days in a suburb west of Cleveland. Yes, I know its pre-school but I was held back. Teachers feared that I may have been deaf. I couldn't follow directions and couldn't use scissors correctly. Matter of fact, I used scissors backwards. After repeating pre-school, my elementary years started and they were at a school near the end of my street. For me this was a cool factor because I didn't have to wait for the bus or my parents to pick me up, rather I could just walk to and from school if I wanted. Lets be honest I think I speak for most on this one when I say, "Nobody likes to really take the bus to school do they?"

In this stage of my life, I had the mindset of just about any other kid. I had some big dreams of either to be a professional sports player or to be an astronaut and walk on the moon. It's at this point where I found my love for sports, especially playing basketball, baseball, soccer and football. It was at this stage as well that I myself had no concept of money and didn't know how the world worked. In all honesty I didn't really care. During these years of my life I started struggling with having no friends and being bullied. I was bullied because I was quiet and being that way I guess that makes me an easy target for bullies to pick on. After surviving these rough years and grade levels, I was off to my next transition stage in my life, junior high school.

The junior high years took me on a journey to two different schools. In these schools, I didn't have many friends and was bullied as well. However, I did manage to play basketball, football, and soccer. It wasn't until 8th grade, where I was diagnosed with ADD/ADHD. My study habits and school skills changed after the diagnosis and for the better. Before I knew it, I began getting high grades in all my subjects. Just when I got a nice rhythm going for this grade level, it was time for me to start my high school life.

My high school stage began and I really didn't make that many friends and was bullied by many, throughout the 4 years. These years weren't as bad though. I went to dances with a girl as a friend, whom herself, thought honored to be asked by me. I had access to a car, played soccer and football for all four years. I wanted to play basketball but it's a shame because I ran into politics and many know what I mean. All who have been to high school can agree of the fact that all four years just fly by relatively quick.

Before I knew it, I was picking what college I went to. Football being my main sport and kicking my specialty, colleges began to recruit me. After dozens of camps and all the hours of hard work, the process of being selected to a college to play football was about to happen. Before I knew it, I would choose the same university of the one my brother went to in the early 90's. I thought this university would be right for me, given that it was in a small Ohio town.

Little did I know, it would foreshadow what of what was to come of my brief two semesters…evil. I was so excited heading into this period of my life to play football in college and so were family and friends. Turns out the stage I'd be entering into, would be one I would never forget. My first day of college was upon me, I said my goodbye, took to heart the lecture I was given and started what I call "10 Months of Hell".

Chapter 2: So It Begins

No sooner than saying goodbye to the family, I had only fifteen minutes to get to my first class, which was College 101. This was a course that basically explained what to expect during your college career. Being my first college class, I had no idea what to expect but the class went just fine and I handled it as well as I could have hoped for. My teacher was the Dean of Students and I even had some football teammates in the class. Even though I thought those teammates were going to be my friends for the long haul, they would be some of the ones that would haze me.

I headed back to my dorm room to change my clothes. Then it was time to go off to football practice. I arrived to practice full of energy and excitement. Even though my first day of practice was relaxing and full of meetings, I had unknowingly met my future enemies, coaches included.

After a nice night of sleep, my 2nd day of college began and the hazing did as well. I went to the cafeteria for lunch with the team and right away the chaos began. I had received my food and one of the teammates decided to trip me and make me fall on my face. Everyone was laughing at me, coaches included, and nobody came to my rescue. I brushed myself off and went to a table to eat alone. Much to my surprise the kicker and punter came to the table and ate with me. I began to make friends with the two at the table and my nerves started to settle. Lunch was over and it was time for the conditioning test at practice.

This test was very difficult. This was made very clear by players who took it before and coaches who have witnessed it. I tried my hardest to pass it but I was unsuccessful at doing so. Not only was it 90 degrees and sunny, the coaches began to haze and humiliate me in front of my teammates. I thought to myself, "What is going on? This is not what I signed up for." It was one thing for me to get hazed but it's a completely different aspect when you get hazed by coaches.

I can remember getting ready to run the length of the field only to be tripped and pushed from behind by two coaches. This made me be last to finish the 100 yards. As I got to the other end of the field, the Head Coach Elliot screamed at me.

"Your fat a** doesn't move fast enough for me. So the next time you are last, I'm going to break your f****** leg!" He yelled forcefully at me.

At this point, I knew the entire team was going to laugh and indeed they did. I felt lost and confused. I didn't understand why I was the target of their hazing. This first day of practice was humiliating and it wouldn't get much better.

After the conditioning test, which I failed, it was time for individual drills. I went with the two kickers to the kicking field. On the field I ended up being made fun of by them for no reason but I didn't think much of it other than joking.

We warmed up for 30 minutes and the special teams unit came to the field for special teams work. The team ran to the field. I was already there and as they came they ran me over. One player speared me and about 20 others stepped on me. As I was in pain, the coaches and players just stood there laughing and didn't say a word. I picked myself up, thriving in pain, and acted like I was okay even though I wasn't. Again I thought to myself, "This is not what I signed up for nor is it

what a football team is supposed to do to fellow
teammates."

I no sooner got done with this thought to
hear Coach Elliot call my name. He told me to
come in and kick a field goal. Well one ball turned
into five balls kicked and all five split the uprights.
This really made me happy and was encouraging at
this point, but this did not sit well with the "hazers".

Every time I made one of those kicks I got
speared by a teammate and coaches just let it
happen. Practice ended and it was off to the locker
room, where not to my surprise more uncomfortable
things began to happen.

Some examples were: being shoved into a
locker, a player telling me he's going to light me up,

teammates questioning me about my sexual orientation and etc.

I finally got out of the locker room and headed back to the dorms. I just wanted to go to bed. Of course I got back to my room and had to talk to my mother on the phone. She wanted to keep up with how my college was going.

The conversation I had with her was quick and not colorful. Wanting to get to bed, I told her everything was going great, even though things were not. A week goes by and the hazing of me stayed the same and didn't stop. I kept telling my mom everything was fine but again it wasn't.

As the second week started, I got ready to go to my Monday morning class. Just then I got a phone call from my mom. She informs me that my dad's father passed away. She said she would be there in the afternoon to pick me up.

I informed my teachers and coaches. Much to my surprise, the football coaches were sympathetic. The coaches told me to take as much time off from football as I needed. Some of the players found out about the news, even though there were only about five of them, they were sympathetic as well.

After a long afternoon, I gathered my things to take home with me. My mother was there to pick me up because my father was with his family getting the funeral arrangements together. As I was picked up, my mother already noticed I was a little bit larger than when she had last seen me. Indeed I had packed on some pounds due to the hazing; just as well as anybody else would in that situation.

I can remember her asking me if everything was okay and this continued the entire two hour car ride home. As much as I wanted to say something about everything that was going on, I couldn't speak about it. The only response I had to her repeated questions was, "Yes, everything is fine; I am having a lot of fun." Saying this to her was the only way to just forget about what was happening, even though saying I was fine couldn't have been any further from the truth.

At last, I arrived home and to the only sign of peace I had seen in two long weeks; my dog.

Whitley was a loving Havanese. The only thing I wanted to do was just spend that day and night relaxing and sleeping. I did just that. The next day was the viewing for my grandpa and the looks I got from a few relatives about my appearance were stunning. Everyone began asking why I looked a little different, and by different, they meant heavier. Again, hiding the truth I told everyone I was fine and had to continue saying that the entire week I was home.

I thought to myself, "How does anyone expect me to explain the terror and hell that is going on." The weeks of the funeral came and went but not without half the United States losing power because of whatever reason which I can't remember.

Before I knew it, the week was over and I was headed back to school. I just wanted to give up, given all the hazing going on. I knew that my crazy college life would continue and probably not get any better when I returned. When I got back to school things only were about to get worse for me and the hazing and bullying was about to intensify.

Chapter 3: Nothing Changes

I arrived back on campus and it was right to football for me. So I walked down to the building where the football meetings were held. There, I was met by coaches and some players whom were sympathetic on the loss of my Grandpa. I learned quickly though that the majority of the team thought otherwise of me going home for the funeral.

I was told from multiple players, "You are a coward for leaving and going home for a stupid funeral. You are lying about that and just wanted to get away from what we are doing to you."

Ethan, on of the team captains, said, "You just went home to get away from us. Your Grandpa never died, you are lying about that and I know it.

You knew it was what we call 'Freshman Hazing Week', and that is why you missed. Seeing you missed, I am going to make your life more hell than you can imagine. The hazing we did last week to the freshman is nothing compared to what I am going to have in store for you. You think the team was nasty to you before you left for a week; well you have another thing coming. I have wanted to hurt you in every way possible and I am going to do it."

I began to really think to myself what my best option would be as far as football. I decided to just play things out. I was scared for the times ahead, but I decided to just move forward and take more of the punishment. I thought I would be respected more. Practice began in the weight room and I can remember doing some pull down exercises. My first set I just did a few, kind of to warm up my arms. I saw Coach Elliot walk over to me and shout,"You only did five… I see girls that do more than you!" The entire team got a laugh out of that comment.

Completely embarrassed, I moved to another area of the room to get in some quick dumbbell work. I started doing my exercises and I was confronted by a captain of the team. Keep in mind he was about six inches taller than me and I am only 5'6".

He denied me my spot to workout in and said to me, "You better move out of my way, I am the captain and what I say goes…If you don't move, I'm going to beat the living hell out of you."

So I responded with, "No, I am not moving, I was here first. I don't care who you are. You should start acting like a captain instead of an a**."

Tension was mounting between us. Then Coach Frank, whom recruited me, came over and stood between us. He said, "Adam you should listen to your captain."

I said, "Only I will listen if he has good advice."

The captain then said, "Coach, can I please destroy Adam and hit him with a dumbbell?"

I thought my coach would stick up for me after he said that. What Frank said to me in response infuriated me to the point where I just blew. My coach proceeded to say, "Sure you absolutely can hit him with a dumbbell....in fact I will applaud you for doing it."

The next thing that came out of my mouth was probably one of the harshest things I have ever said during the entire time of being hazed at this school. "You hit me with that dumbbell then you better make sure I don't get up.... If I get up after, it's going to be me making your life a living hell instead of you or anyone on this team doing it to me."

After a long moment of silence, Coach Frank took me into his office by the arm. He said I was out of control and I should have expected the hazing and harassment because I was a freshman. He told me that I would have to be a man and just stand up to what is going on. I was told if I couldn't handle this, maybe I should just transfer to the school I was originally going to go to. He mentioned to me that he has connections with that particular school. I began to think why I would believe this man, especially after he had just said it was okay for a teammate to virtually knock me unconscious. Also this man has lied to me since day one of recruiting me. He proceeded to tell me that the main reason for being upset is because of the grieving process and not the hazing.

He said, "Adam, the hazing shouldn't bother you at all and you are mentally unstable because you can't handle it. Now get your f***** a** out of my office and go down to the practice field for practice."

I walked out of the office and the two kickers were waiting for me to go to practice. All I said was, "Lets go."

We walked out to the car and in complete silence headed to practice. With the two kickers looking on in concern for me, they asked if everything was okay. I told them, "Yeah I am okay."

We made it to the practice field and I rushed out of the car, went in the locker room and got dressed as quickly as I could. Off to the field I trotted, alone I might add, and started to warm up. With less than a week to go before our first game, I knew I had to be focused and ready to impress. Distractions at this point, I knew were going to be disastrous in proving to the coaches I should be the kicker. It was game week and I needed to make the dress list, as it was an away game and the coaches could only dress a certain amount of players.

Almost an hour after warming up, the team arrived and practice began. I quickly observed I wasn't in the mix to get a chance to prove myself. The entire practice I wasn't even used as kicker, rather I was someone the team could use basically as a tackling dummy. I was used in drills holding tackling bags for teammates to practice on. Instead of hitting the bags, teammates decided to use me to hit. I guess a football drill isn't complete at this particular university until I have been hit, I thought to myself.

Hiding the pain, I kept getting up and tried to show my toughness. Practiced ended but night meetings for football were to take place shortly after on the main campus. Even during these meeting at night, players once again used the time to crack jokes and be cruel to me. Of course I should have known that something embarrassing was going to happen and it did. At the end of the night the freshman were supposed to perform skits in front of the team as part of a so called "fun activity".

Fun it was, for everyone else except me. I wasn't told anything about the skits because I was gone for a funeral. I was told to sing the alma mater of the university and to perform the part of a male stripper. When I refused to do any of this I was booed and yelled at by players and coaches. Amongst the laughter as well, teammates of mine came from behind me on stage and threw me off and to the ground. Hurt I was, but I picked myself from the ground and walked back to my room in tears.

The following day practice started and it was time for everyone to check the dress list to see if they would be traveling to the road game. Down

the list I looked for my name but it was nowhere to

be found.

Chapter 4: Broken Heart

I was so broken hearted that I didn't find my name on the dress list. It was tough to hide my emotions; let alone I had to hide them the entire practice. To say that I was crushed at this point was an understatement.

As practice went on, tears kept running down my face. They were quickly wiped away by me because I didn't want flack for crying. The other two kickers Billy and Jake however noticed I was visibly upset.

I simply told them, "I am upset for not making the dress list."

Their response to me was, "Keep your head up kid and keep working hard."

I thought to myself that the situation I was in was similar to that of the famous football movie we all know and love. Practice ended and the three of us went to the car and I was in complete silence again. As we headed for the dorms my eyes were so watery, I felt that there was going to be a flood.

I got to my room, closed the door and called my family to tell them the news. Telling them I wasn't going to be on the dress list really sickened me. Thinking that my family would be sympathetic, they were not. In fact, they could have cared less even though I was crying. I guess I was hoping for some comfort but I guess that was not true with my family. Down to my friends room I went so I could have someone to talk to.

Before I could say anything, he and his girlfriend asked me what was wrong. I tried to get a word out but I couldn't. With tears building up, I had to let them go. Crying so hard, my body collapsed in sadness. As I fell, his girlfriend caught me and I held my face to cry in her arms. Whatever I did to stop the crying, it wouldn't work for a good twenty minutes. The day I was having seemed so endless because of the shock, the only thing I wanted to do was go to bed. With class over for the week, I decided to go to bed even though it was early evening.

After a long night sleeping, I still woke up sad because I knew I wouldn't be dressing for game day. To make matters worse my mother insisted on picking me up to drive me to the game, even though I didn't want to go. To be reluctant was the first thing that came to my mind. I guess we as humans are forced to do things that we heavily don't agree with in life.

On the way to the game that night we found ourselves lost because of some bad directions. At the point of being lost, I was laughing inside because I thought that may have been a sign that I shouldn't be at the game to watch. Of course I really didn't have a say, but for some reason my mother and sister did.

At the same time, I heard both of them ask, "Don't you think it's a great to go and cheer your teammates on? Don't you think you should be there, after all you are a player on the team?"

I lashed back and said, "Team, what team and what players? If you had any clue about what is happening you would understand why I say that!" All was silent after I said that for at least a good twenty minutes, from what I remember.

We finally made it to the game and our team was nearly down twenty points early in the second quarter. So I thought to myself, "Man what a great time to arrive. My team is down by twenty and I just wonder how many points we can manage to lose by."

I know many of you reading this are thinking why such harsh thinking but come on, can you really blame me? As our team and opponent traded scores before half, I felt as though momentum was starting to shift back toward us. It was not hard to imagine the halftime speech our head coach had for our team as well as other coaches, nor did I want to be in the locker room to hear it as well. Not having a lot off offensive weapons on the team, made it hard for us to make a comeback. Sure we had a big quarterback with a big arm, decent running back and a future two time football world champ in Mason, but far from that making mistakes just killed us on this night.

Though we had improved our play in the second half and even made it a game, we just couldn't muster up enough stops defensively or scores offensively for the comeback. Much to the delight of the crowd we had lost to our cross-town rivals. All I could think about is how hard practice would be to begin the following week.

Chapter 5: I Can't Take It

As any team knows, no matter the sport, losing isn't fun. When you play hard though, coaches have a tendency to cut some slack and work on things that need to be improved. This is what happened in our team's case.

As Monday practice started, the only thing that happened was a team meeting to talk about the previous game and upcoming week ahead. At the end of the meeting Coach Elliot said, "If we can have a great week of practice then come Friday, instead of a walkthrough, we will go to the park pool to hang out with the public."

The whole room erupted in cheer, and even I cracked a smile believe it or not. Tuesday practice seemed to go fine but of course the day wasn't over. A team meeting was called for nighttime in a building just outside my dorm. The building we went into turned out to be the library. Here as a team, we talked about study tables which were designed to get our homework done with tutors. Everyone was assigned their days and that was it.

The team went outside with coaches for a brief special teams meeting. I got to be with the First Team for once, though it was a run through. Of course with everything else up to this point, the upper classman harassed me.

Ethan, a senior whom really hated me, shouted to coach Frank "This j****** isn't going to be out there with us come game day is he?"

Coach Frank responded, "No, us coaches will make sure that he isn't." The meeting ended and I went back to my room in disgust.

Once again I got treated with disrespect from my teammates and coaches. These individuals continued to get away with such heinous acts and my hands were really tied because I was getting scared in the violent situation.

As practice approached for Wednesday and Thursday, kickers were allowed to practice at the stadium because of a home game. It was such a relief for me because I knew my teammates wouldn't be around to hurt me during practice. Seeing the stadium was great because it meant I would be dressing for the game that week because the rules for the league allowed all players to dress for their respective home games.

After two fun days of kicking, Friday was here and though I thought the pool sounded great, my team and coaches, go figure, would turn the day into a nightmare for me.

Chapter 6: Chaos at Its Best

Lets be honest, no matter how confident someone is, many of us in this world are not in one certain area; going to the pool, stripping down to our swim gear and showing off our bodies as we go for a swim. Well no surprise here that I am one of those people. What was about to happen didn't help this matter either.

On a bright sunny day in early fall, we as a football team, arrived at the local pool for a swim meet and greet with the local community. Into the pool area I walked with my other kicking friends and we found a spot on a small hill near the pool. The rest of my teammates wasted no time finding their spots to sit and hopped right in the pool.

Myself on the other hand, took my time because I didn't feel comfortable hopping in the pool. So there I sat watching, with my shirt and sunglasses on. It took only five minutes to hear the whispers about me. So I figured what the hell, I might as well jump in and await what punishment or foolish things the team would do to me while in the pool.

Seconds after jumping in, I was cornered by a few players. Slowly but surely I was trapped without an escape route. They circled me like a school of fish or hungry sharks. A quick punch and elbow to the face was what I got and they were happy about doing it to me. Amazing how nobody saw it, coaches included had their backs turned, as if it were planned. You would figure the lifeguard would do something but, he was looking a different way attending to a different situation.

On I swam to somewhere different in the pool where two assistants James and Richard were. Though I didn't think anything of seeing them, Richard had put his arm around me. Only seconds later he was trying to force my head under water and hold it there, virtually trying to drown me.

Richard in the mean time blocked the view of others from seeing this. My only option of getting my head above water was to punch and grab Richard where it hurt the most. So I punched and grabbed down below and Richard had no choice but to let go of his hold. Up from the water I sprang

and swam out of the pool.

From the pool, I grabbed my clothes and cell

phone. I decided to quickly dial for a cab to pick

me up. As I escaped that team gathering without

any notice, I thought this was going to be the

smartest thing; of course I was wrong as teammates

of mine would punish me for it later that night.

Stunned by what happened, I gathered my thoughts

in my room while shaking because yes, I was afraid.

Chapter 7: Getting Worse

Upset and in shock, I went to the cafeteria to eat but really had no idea why because I wasn't hungry. Not feeling very well, the only thing I was able to eat was a salad. I was usually a salad eater but I just was too overwhelmed by my feelings to finish the salad. Not being able to finish my meal, I had left the cafeteria and headed toward my room.

I sat quietly for the next few hours gathering my thoughts on how I was being treated. Before I knew it, the day turned into early evening. Thinking that the night couldn't get any worse or scary it did. A violent knock on my door came and deep voiced words followed.

Words spoken were, "Open the door now!"

I quickly thought to myself, now who could this be and what do they want.

I answered the door to linebacker Ethan and he said, "You should never leave anything early and because of that you missed a team function at the junkyard. We were going to haze and beat you there. So just wait, you are not going to dream about what is in store for you next. So sleep tight and see you at pre-game meal in the morning."

Infuriated I was, I slammed my door shut, turned off my lights and went to bed.

Chapter 8: First Game

I awoke the next morning angry about what happened the previous night but excited deep down because this was the day I dressed for a college football team. To the pre –game meal I went and Coach Elliot had a message for our team. He says, "I spoke to the opposing coach this week and he lacks respect for our team. So being that our game will be on the national score alert because of who we are playing, lets show them how to play tough nosed football and embarrass them."

Fired up we all were, we ate our breakfast and then drove to the practice field to get dressed for the game. Once there, the three kickers were able to leave as soon as we were ready because it took us a little longer to warm up. Off we went to the stadium for the very first time.

Upon arrival, fans were tailgating and ringing cowbells as we got out of the car. This was pretty exciting to be dressed and have fans acknowledge us as we walked into the stadium. So for a brief period of time I was able to be happy. This would be short lived though because what I was about to be told, put anger back inside me. Coach Frank and Perry came with the team bus and noticed me warming up.

At the same time, both coaches shouted. "Why in the hell are you warming up? So you really think you are playing today? Make yourself useful and go shag footballs for your friends because that is all you are worth to this team!"

Though angry, I followed orders and did what I was asked. After about thirty minutes of warm ups, it was kickoff time. As the game unfolded, the team was hitting on all cylinders and we were blowing our opponent out of the water. Being that we were putting the game out of reach, I thought I would get the chance to play. As the clock and quarters winded down, I realized I just wasn't going to get in.

The game ended and I was probably the least satisfied person, even though we had won. One victory speech by our head coach, and an invite to a party later on that evening, I was on my way to

a night I wouldn't forget.

Chapter 9: Unforgivable Night

So let me just admit that for the vast majority of college students, being away from home meant drinking at college regardless if of age or not. I for one was no different in drinking of adult beverages. In knowing I was away from home, I planned on drinking but not as much as it would turn out to be. Realizing it was wrong, I unexpectedly did it more because the problems with hazing I was going through. I thought by drinking, the issue on my mind of being hazed was going to fade, but on this night and many others, drinking opened up a "can of worms".

I would have normally gone home on weekends but after a big win I figured I would stay behind to celebrate. Dressed for a night out on the town with Billy and Jake, I headed to Billy's room. Once there, the three of us headed to Billy's car to drive to get beer and some fast food. After getting those items, we headed to Billy's room to eat, drink and chat about the day's game and the big win we had. It was a fun time while it lasted and I thought the night was going to go great but I was wrong. In fact actions of what happened on this night might surprise some and might not.

Off we went to my friend Chad's house. He lived near the railroad track, which was not too far from our team weight room. In the house the three of us walked and about five other teammates were there. In a hurry my teammate's actions got out of hand against me. I noticed a funny smell as I walked in to a cloud of smoke. I realized it wasn't cigarettes either; it was weed, as those college students called it.

I was punched by someone, blindfolded by another and then forced to smoke the weed. Pissed off I was, I sat down and drank some beer, just to act like I was having fun. About five beers later, I was soon blindfolded again and dragged to the upstairs only to be thrown into a room that was very dark. The blindfold was taken off my eyes and the television turned on to a porn movie.

A teammates voice, though blinded by the darkness, I couldn't tell who it was, says, "If you don't watch this movie till its over and try to escape this room without being told you will be beaten."

About ten minutes later I picked myself up from the corner of the room, where I had been sitting and found my way to the door. I tried to escape but quickly found myself wrapped in the arms of two masked men, which were from the football team. These two masked men proceeded to take me and toss me from an upstairs window, where I luckily landed in a bush. Thankfully the bush was strong enough to kind of break my fall and the house wasn't that large otherwise I might have wound up dead. Scraped up I was, it took me a good five minutes, maybe more, to come to my senses.

When I did come to my senses, I decided if my teammates were trying to kill me or severely injure me, why let them, rather I would just try myself. I felt that for me, the least painful way would be the railroad tracks up the road, about 2,000 feet from where I was standing. Once I walked to the tracks, I stood and waited….waited… and waited some more. Knowing that this train came by more often than not and hadn't shown up when I was there turned out ironic for me.

Fifteen minutes and no train in sight, I stepped off the tracks, realizing that no train coming meant it wasn't meant for me to end my life. "The man upstairs" had other plans for me in mind that was far better, even though I had no idea what.

Chapter 10: No Focus

As if things couldn't get any worse with football, they were getting worse in the classroom. I began getting homework and tests back with failing grades instead of passing. To make things worse, study tables at night with part of the football team weren't much better. Not only players but coaches such like Coach Perry and Coach James, began calling me things like "retarded", "dumb", and "mentally incompetent".

Feeling helpless and defenseless, I gathered myself and belongings after only an hour of these study tables and headed back to my dorm room. Being that upset I felt my room was going to be the safest place to go and that is where I went. As I hopped in bed for the night I said to myself, "Just what the hell is going to happen next?"

I could sniff it, something was going to happen and nothing good was going to come of it. Of course what was about to happen later that night would happen multiple times throughout the next two months.

Chapter 11: Painful

As I recall, I had shut my lights and television off pretty early and went to bed. During the night on campus throughout the year, the university had their version of security that patrolled the campus at night. The group was strongly dedicated to students in the criminal justice program. If students were to work, they could use it as credit hours toward his or her degree. Of course, I was wrong to figure that not one of the football players were in this group, let alone a handful. I found this out the hard and abusing way. Sometime in the middle of the night, I heard my door creek open.

Busting into my room, flipping on the lights, I rolled and saw men with ski-like masks. I wasn't sure what was going on but soon I heard similar voices to ones that I heard on the football field. Putting two and two together I knew it was teammates of mine. Within seconds, about five of them were on top of me, beating me with what I believe was a small chain. While beating me I was informed to say or scream nothing, so I did as informed.

What I found strange was after the beating was over, I noticed the only thing bloody was my black under gear I wore. My face was not touched, so I felt at least this attack was pre-meditated. Not hitting me in the face meant no visual evidence of a beating. My second question I thought to myself was how did these masked men get into my room? I have always wondered if somehow a duplicate key was made but I was never able to solve that mystery. The only other options I thought were it was my RA involved or maybe these security people, who were from the football team, had keys to everyone around campus, in case of emergency.

When I awoke the next morning, my skin was bloodied and stuck to my under gear. The only option I had was to get up and go to class, then go to football and act as if everything was fine. Showing that I was in pain, I felt the hazers would thrive off of it and my situation would only worsen if I showed it. With that being said, my day began and it would turn out to be about the same as the

day before…bad!

A person can only take so much abuse until

there is no use anymore of being beat down by any

bully. That's what they love and thrive off of and

that's exactly what the coming days had in store for

me.

Chapter 12: No Use, Just Abuse!

While I did go to class, the day seemed so miserable because the pain I was in. The failing grades I was getting back were no help either. All day I thought to myself that if hazing is coming to the point of beating then either; I hoped they don't kill me or I will do it myself if the first option did not happen on its own.

I know many are thinking why think that but at that point my mind was so off because of the beatings I didn't know where to run or who to talk to. Anything I said to anyone got back to me and made the situation worse, it was like my conversations with anyone were being tapped into all the time.

By the time I was done contemplating this, classes were done and I was headed to football. Sad to say but I only recall one thing that happened at practice on that day and it was nothing of any good. I and the other two kickers decided to head to the practice field early on that day. Once there, two of the graduating assistant coaches were in the locker room when we got there. Coach Richard was one of the coaches and the other was Coach Ed doing some work for the football team. Richard decided that he was going to question me on my sexual orientation and sexual trivia in general. Then, with Coach Ed taking a shower, Richard decided to throw a football behind the walls of the shower and into the area where he was standing.

Coach Richard proceeded to say, "Adam, I want you to go hop in the shower with Coach Ed. While you are in there, I want you to tell him that you have been ordered by me to rub him down everywhere on his body!"

Though I did what I was told and went into the shower, the coach thankfully told me to promptly leave but not before chuckling. Practice came and went and I left with my dignity, swallowed and thought how it was going to be when I was about to go try and end my life for a second time.

I first started my night by eating a salad in the cafeteria. I think it was my nerves of wanting to try again but I got sick from eating it. The way I

72

thought of ending my life was to poison myself with alcohol. Being underage I had to have one of my friends that were old enough to by me the beer. Once getting it I was dropped off at the back door of the dorm building, where I snuck it in via my backpack. The night I was about to have was not only disgusting from my standpoint but from the hazers as well.

Chapter 13: Second Attempt

As no surprise to anyone, my thinking of drinking beer this time was to forget about the situation as a whole. Meaning, you guessed it, I tried using the beer to end my life and leave this world.

As I recall, I began drinking my case of beer and I was not wasting my time with each can. After like six beers in an hour, my body started to feel the effects. About an hour later I had, I think, fifteen in my system and my dorm room was spinning out of control. I can remember a knock at my door and two of my rare friends on the team, came in my room with a beer bong. With me virtually passed out on my bed, just moments after I shut the door, my friend Phillip and his buddy bonged the rest of my beer I had.

Thinking I had been passed out for a while, I felt a tap on my shoulder. Dazed and confused I noticed it was Phillip, even though my vision was blurred and I was spinning. What he told me, surprised me a great deal and I didn't know and still don't know how it was possible. Phillip had said I'd thrown up in the hallway and that I should go clean it up before getting into some serious trouble. So staggering I went down the hall to clean up my vomit.

What was even more disheartening is a line of students in the hallway laughing at me as I struggled. After the clean up I headed right for the bathroom and what happened there would be just as if not more devastating.

Vomiting and going to the bathroom simultaneously was no easy task. What was more embarrassing is the fact that this struggling moment was being caught by photographs from football players who followed me in there and I wasn't aware. I didn't know of any photographing until the next day. What I remember from the rest of the night was crying for any help because I thought the drinking was actually going to end up killing me, I was extremely sick! I don't remember how long it had taken me to fall asleep because of the spinning but I did and did so in the fact of not knowing if I was going to wake up the next morning.

76

The morning came and I had awoke to the morning sun. Somehow I made it to the school building that morning for class. As I arrived, I found something so sickening it made me not even go to class. I found students laughing at me for some reason and when I researched some more about what exactly was happening I found pictures hanging outside the building. These pictures were of me from the night before on the toilet and being sick. Multiple people took pictures of this event and had posted them on the school building. Even as I walked inside, they were posted on the wall. Faculty at this point were so lackluster and unaware they said nothing about the photos as if they had no interest or didn't care what was going on.

Embarrassed I was at the amount of people

pointing, laughing and starring I quickly turned out

of the building running back to my dorm where I

slammed my door shut!

Chapter 14: Continued Abuse

My abuse from players, coaches, and students would continue the rest of the semester and next. With masks on, players would come to my room at night and beat me until bloodied. I remained silent during these beatings just hoping that one day they would stop.

In one circumstance I was blindfolded, driven in a car near some cornfield and shot by a real gun at point blank range. The bullet missed me by inches but was so close I could feel the heat of it. Party after party I was forced to go to, more abuse came with it and led to more aggravation. These parties included having photos taken of me again and being posted in the main school building.

In another party I was forced to do a shot of basically pure alcohol and it almost made me stop breathing. As I asked for help, players and some coaches laughed at me.

In the same party I was speared through a couch by linebacker Ethan. As he did I can remember him saying "I have been meaning to do that to you for a long time!"

The only way I was able to stop the hazing from happening was to change dorm rooms my second semester and so I did and moved in with a friend of mine. Although he didn't know my situation, week after week I continued to get beer and just drink the semester away, barely attending class.

Finally the second semester saw me quit football because I had had enough and I eventually even failed out of college, and that is the way my first year of college went.   It also had me find out the one of my great friends had tragically passed away in an auto accident, you know who you are and you will be missed. (The following chapter will be the conclusion and final thoughts, so please, I ask all reading to pay attention).

Chapter 15: Concluding Thoughts

Pictured below is me, the author…Adam Sand.

I end this book sort of abruptly but with great pride and joy to be telling you my story and how I have survived hazing. My hope is that this book helps at least one person and stops them from being a victim of hazing or bullying. Just by writing the book I feel I have won the "war against hazing and bullying".

Without further ado, I ask all victims of such heinous acts to stand up and fight for our rights! Should this book do well I am looking at speaking about all incidents and stopping hazing from happening anywhere as much as I can influence. To end this book with peace and so many more questions I am sure that will be answered if asked, is a great accomplishment. Some things are better to be said in person about incidents then in a book.

Stopping hazing is going to be hard but it starts with the laws. As of now, the laws protect the criminals more so than the do the victims and until that's changed many other laws will not be resolved regardless of who is in charge. Statue of limitations vary for some reason from state to state, why this is, is beyond me.

A last thought of mine is I hope this book bids well for others and hope it benefits people from reading it.

For the Hazers and Bullies out there: "We, the victims are more united now than ever, and we will overcome your antics someday!" For the victims like me, just keep on going, good things will come of it. Look at me, I found a beautiful wife; I have close friends whom are very important to me and I found other activities such as riding roller coasters. I set personal goals to reach while riding roller coasters, which is one of my many favorite hobbies. Activities like this in the world make you feel free and the hazing and bullying does not exist.

About The Author

For me, Adam Sand, writing this book was hard. In fact if I had not met my wife Cathy at the local amusement park, I wouldn't be here telling you this story today. She saw something special in me, believed in me and for once I really felt wanted by someone. I assume many wonder about some details in this book if they appear to be vague, well as the saying goes "some things are better left unsaid". Although I am sure that if questioned more about these certain events I will explain in detail.

As far as where I am from, well I grew up in a suburb of Cleveland and now live closer to my favorite thrill park with my wife and step-daughter.

As said before without the help of my wife and step-daughter, this book would have never been made, so a lot people including myself should thank them.

It may seem hard for some to read this book and I apologize. Just know that I suffer from PTSD because of the hazing and I have Aspergers as well, so as some might imagine, it was hard to finish the book. Please enjoy this book and learn from the effects hazing has on someone. I hope it bids well and look forward to meeting potential avid readers and fans of this book. Thanks again and enjoy!

Made in the USA
Middletown, DE
31 May 2017